Patient Prayers

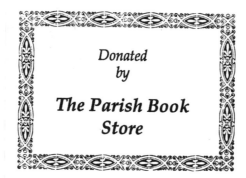

John V. Chervokas

Patient Prayers

TALKING TO GOD
FROM A HOSPITAL BED

Crossroad · New York

1989

The Crossroad Publishing Company
370 Lexington Avenue, New York, N.Y. 10017

Copyright © 1989 by John V. Chervokas

Printed in the United States of America

Library of Congress Cataloging-in-Publication Data

Chervokas, John, 1936–
    Patient prayers: talking to God from a hospital
bed/John V. Chervokas.
        p.   cm.
    ISBN 0-8245-0943-9
    1. Sick—Prayer-books and devotions—English.
I. Title.
BV4910.C47   1989
242'.86—dc19   89-615
                                                   CIP

Contents

Foreword

When we are forced to be confined to a hospital, whether it is for a short time or for a few weeks, our natural inclination is to lie there and brood. That is understandable. Fear and pain breed brooding.

Certainly we are concerned about our health and, if we are not talking about it to the medical staff or to our visitors, some of us might already be talking about it, wittingly or unwittingly, to God . . . as in, "Oh, God, when will they take the cast off?" or "God, do I still need this IV in my arm?"

Yet the time we spend thinking about *our* specific problem while in the hospital might be better spent by talking to God about the perceptions and incidents, the feelings and the people who affect and enliven, disturb and enlighten our hospital stay. These kinds of conversations serve two very useful purposes: one, they usually take our minds off our reason for being in the hospital in the first place and, two, they expand our appreciation of God's eternally intriguing world, our relationship *to* it, and our role *in* it.

Just how difficult is it to break the ice? How tough is

it initiating a dialogue with God? Not all that difficult if we are honest and open and humble. Oh yes, if there is one thing we are sure to get out of our hospital stay, it's a heightened sense of humility.

Here, then, are some thoughts God has heard from hospital beds. They may or may not be similar to notions that have come into *your* mind, too, during a period of recuperation. If you are reading this while you are actually *in* a hospital bed, consider the capacity this incapacitation has afforded you to open up a new and direct communication channel to the Creator. Leap at the chance. No, at second thought, don't leap. Raising the level of your bed a wee bit will suffice.

The "What's My Angle?" Prayer

Every time I've called, someone's come,
on the walk or on the run
to crank me up or down
into a different position.
Still I am not completely satisfied.
Why not?
What is it I want, God?
What is it I'm looking for?
A better angle to watch TV?
A more comfortable position
to sip my ginger ale
without spilling any?
A more upright posture
to greet my visitors
with a semblance of vigor?
Or . . .
or am I simply craving
what just about everyone
You ever created
is craving?
You know what that is:
a little attention.

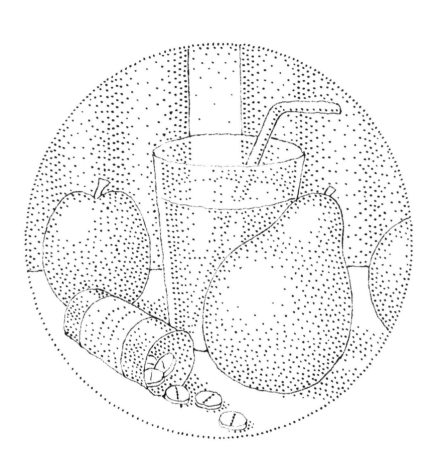

Pillows and Pills, Tissues and Straws. In most environments items such as these would be considered commonplace. They would be considered commonplace, that is, if anyone gave them a moment of consideration in the first place. Most of us probably wouldn't even bother. Yet, when we look at the most ordinary items from our hospital bed, these otherwise insignificant things take on almost heroic qualities.

From our vantage (if that's an appropriate term) point, we tend to stare at these commonplace items. We fumble with them. We arrange them. We *re-*arrange them. Cezanne could not have spent as much time and psychic energy on his still life subjects as we do with the still life objects nearby.

And to what end? For what useful purpose? Why are we prone (quite literally prone) to gaze for long stretches of time at the box of tissues, the bent straw, yes, even the emesis basin?

Well, for one thing the act of staring has somewhat of a tranquilizing effect. That blank stare at the pear a visitor left us can be very sedating. (Did Cezanne ever fall asleep staring at one of *his* pears?) But more than that, staring at commonplace items can be a source, a springboard, a conversational cue to pursue a thought or a meditation.

These basic, and somewhat banal, objects on the table near our bed, on chairs and window sills around our bed, even sometimes *on* the bed itself, can be thought of as "reflectibles." We stare at them and we reflect upon them. And, of course, we can also share that reflection in a prayer. Take the straw, for example.

The Straw Prayer

"Little sips," the nurse tells me,
"take little sips of juice,"
as if I never had a straw
between my lips before.
Speedy slurping, at my age, isn't very attractive
and not all that easy to manage;
little sips are about as much
as I can handle anyway.
And I must tell you, God,
little sips are just fine with me.
In fact, the "little sips" of life,
the brief passing pleasures, the simple joys,
are a constant reminder that this straw of life
I've been blessed with is a truly wondrous gift.
So I thank You for this gift,
and *will* thank You for this gift
with each and every "little sip" I take.

The "Curtain Call" Prayer

The nurse pulls back the curtain
that separates my bed from the others
with such gusto and panache.
What does she expect?
Does she want me to
sit up and take a bow?
Well, maybe I should.
After all, I've been cleaned up for company.
I'm ready to receive the world.
Why shouldn't I take a "curtain call"?
Perhaps, God, this business
of putting on a "new me"
isn't as difficult as I thought.
Maybe it just requires a yank
of the draperies around my bed,
or pulling open the shower curtain
before I step out,
or raising the window shade
in the morning . . .
and ta-dah! . . .
there's a "new me,"
a kinder, more caring, more thoughtful me,
a me more in tune with what You expect me to be.
I know, I know, it's not that easy, God,
but with Your help I'll remember
that the potential is always there
for a "new me" to appear
every time a curtain is pulled open.

The ID Band Prayer

What a perfect reminder of just
how all-knowing You are,
a fact, like some other facts about You
I, sometimes inadvertently,
   sometimes conveniently,
forget.
This piece of plastic around my wrist,
this band, this bracelet,
must stay with me
as long as I'm here.
It identifies me;
it prevents me
from being mistaken
for some other patient
in the hospital.

Yet, You never confuse me
with any one of the billions
of beings on earth.
You recognize me as singular, unique,
unlike any other person You have ever created.
You've always known that
and *will* always know that.
What a wonderfully consoling thought it is
to know I won't need
an ID band in eternity!

The "Why Flowers?" Prayer

God, why have You put the bug in people's heads
to bring flowers to us in hospitals?
No matter how glorious
the flowers at first may be,
they soon shrivel and wilt
on our tables and sills.
Can we, who are concerned
about shriveling
and wilting ourselves,
really be cheered
by a vaseful of fading flowers?
Couldn't You suggest something
more upbeat for visitors to bring?
Something, perhaps, that reminds us
of the heavenly life You've promised us,
rather than something that reflects
the relative brevity of this one?

Thermometer Meditation

When I was a child it seemed I had to hold
the thermometer under my tongue forever
until the red fluid—or was it silver?—
told my mother
precisely how feverish I was.
Today, the nurse comes around
with one of those instant thermometers,
dips it into my mouth, and quickly out,
and takes a reading in no time at all.

Come to think of it, God,
isn't that the way I tend to judge people . . .
instantly,
in a flash,
right away?
Have you crafted me
into such a precise instrument
that I am actually able
to take an accurate reading
of my fellow human being
in just a few seconds?

Or . . . or . . .
am I being unfair
with my snap judgments,
my hasty opinions?
As a child, I held my tongue still,
realizing it would take some time
to get an accurate reading.
As an adult, perhaps I should
hold my tongue still, too,
and for the very same reason.

The Mystery Veggie Meditation

I've pushed it around,
I've poked and I've probed
and I still haven't the foggiest idea
what this mashed up vegetable is.
It's a mystery that
neither my sense of smell
nor my sense of taste
seems capable of solving.

You've blessed me with these senses—
and don't think I'm not grateful, God,
but then You present me
with so many questions
that my blessed senses can't answer.
Oh sure, some of those questions
aren't all that important,
like identifying this mysterious veggie;
but some other questions
that defy my senses
are as important as life itself.
Questions such as:
"who are You?"
and "where are You?"
and "why don't You make Yourself known?"
Tell me, good God, are we really better off
having to wrestle with mysteries like these?

Library Cart Meditation

Although I don't want to be here
any longer than I have to,
I must confess
when the library cart rattles by
I think about a lifetime
of lazing and lolling
and catching up on all
the greatest books ever written
(with a potboiler thrown in
every once in awhile).

Not here, of course, God,
not here.
Maybe on a beach,
or in a shady backyard.
Strange, isn't it, God,
how I constantly complain
about not having the time for this and that?
So then where have all those writers
found the time to write those books
that I can never
seem to find
the time
to read?

A Prayer for Greeting Card Companies

The better writers, it's said, write from experience.
If that's so, and I have no reason to doubt it,
then the people who contrive couplets such as:
 "our sunniest wishes we hasten to send
 hoping you soon will be on the mend"
should check into a hospital right away.

The daisies on the front of the card,
the peaceful pond, the swans, the gentle green hills
suggest a more heartfelt message
would be inside,
something more touching than the trite
"quick-sick,"
"hear-cheer,"
"worse-nurse"
rhymes.

Could You, the source of so much inspiration—
all inspiration many might argue—
shower, if not inspiration,
then a few insightful nuggets
on the people who design,
the writers who write,
the companies that sell
those get well cards?

A Meditation—and Revelation—Induced by Oxygen

Although, thank You, I don't need oxygen
the way a number of my corridor colleagues do,
there might be a few other infusions
which would render me, if not healthier,
then certainly a more bearable human being.

Could I perhaps walk around tugging
a little tank of Good Humor, the tube
from the cylinder to my nose
dispensing a steady stream of optimism
counteracting the gloom that
my own system seems to produce in abundance?

Or what about a metered amount of
Genuine Interest flowing regularly
into my body? On those rare occasions
when I *do* show interest in a person's
opinions my interest usually has an
ulterior motive. A Genuine Interest
machine would make a significant difference.

Then, too, I would surely profit
from a constant supply of Tact,
and a good strong dose to stifle any
bluntness before that hurtful remark
should pass my lips.

Any of these character supplements
flowing into me
would make a better me,
but I hear You, God, I hear You,
—shouldn't I be generating
these admirable qualities on my own?

Meditation While Holding a Toothbrush

Have I brushed my teeth today?
I don't remember.
If I were home, I'd remember.
Brushing teeth at home is important.
More important than brushing teeth here.
Being cheery and bright is important here.
More important here than at home.
Is there a place between home and here
where both brushing teeth
and being cheery and bright
are important?
Why do You suppose this question
just crossed my mind?
Could it be the little pink pills, God?
Do they make me forget to brush my teeth,
but remind me to be bright and cheery?

"The Sides Are Up" Prayer

I trust it's not a reversion
to my crib days, God,
but I must confess it feels so good
to have the sides of my bed
pulled up at night.
I gaze at the bars and,
as my eyes grow heavy,
rather than feeling any cooped-up sensation,
I rest safe and secure and warm.
   With You involved
   in every phase of my life
   I'll strive to remember
   I need never be fearful.
   I'll try not to forget
   that in *Your* loving care
   "the sides" are always up.

Funny Friends and Fidgety Relatives and a wide assortment of old and new acquaintances feel as though they ought to pop in, drop by, say hello. Whether you actually need their dropping by or crave their cheering up is not the issue. People *want* to come and *will* come whether you want them to or not.

Sometimes you will; other times you won't. Yet whatever the situation, whatever your frame of mind on a given day, every time a person comes to visit you in the hospital there is an opportunity for you to include a third party in that visit. What for? Well, maybe it's something your visitor says that will trigger a thought and you want to share that thought with God. Or perhaps it is something your friend or relative brings that will spur a conversation with God. Or it might be something you yourself say and do during visiting hours that you'd like God's opinion on. Then go ahead. Ask it. Latch onto the opportunity. For no matter who pulls up a chair alongside your bed, that Permanent Visitor (the One who doesn't need a pass to get in) is always at hand should you choose to include God into your company.

Prayer for a Well-Meaning Visitor

When I say "she means well"
the phrase probably says more about me
than it does about her.
And what it says about me
isn't all that flattering,
now is it, God?
Because when I say
"she means well"
it's always followed by
one of my critical "buts,"
as in:
"but she talks too much,"
"but she repeats herself,"
"but she doesn't know when to leave."

Help me to remember, dear God,
that the visitor *I* find tiresome,
You find a treasure;
the visitor *I* find boring,
You have blessed
just as wondrously
as *You* have blessed me.

Prayer for a Jogging Chaplain

He comes as a messenger of Your goodness
in an old T-shirt,
raggedy shorts,
and a pair of battered Adidas.
Is he so excited about his message
that he had to tear over here to tell it?
Or is it his customary habit,
after his daily run,
to cool down by offering consolation?
Whatever the case, may it ever be thus.
May this jogger keep jogging
my sleepy conscience,
helping me to sharpen my stride
in this race to eternity.
Amen.

Prayer for a Most Thoughtful Visitor

Bless her for not saying, "You look terrific";
   (I would have to fib back, "I feel pretty good, too")
Bless her for not talking about *her* aches and pains;
   (I sense they are probably more painful than mine)
Bless her for her smile that lights up my room;
   (One of those genuine smiles that are so rare today)
But most of all, God, bless this dear thoughtful soul
                   for sneaking me
                   a corned beef on rye.

Prayer for a Nervous Visitor

He's trying to be casual and matter-of-fact,
but the fact of the matter is he's not.
He sits on my bed, not on the chair,
like a crooner atop a piano.
Yet he can't fool me—
and certainly not You.
He's uncomfortable and it shows.
But uncomfortable with what?
My illness? Me? The room? Himself?
In the few minutes left, God,
before visiting hours are over,
help him appreciate that
what we are doing here,
both he and I,
is participating in one of
life's little glitches.
   And remind him, God,
   that every one of life's glitches
   enriches
   both those living
   and observing
   that life.

Prayer While a Visitor
Watches Me Eat

I haven't had anyone sit and watch me eat
since my father tried to cajole me into carrots
by pretending the spoon holding the puree
was an airplane looking for a hangar.

Now, it seems, a visitor will always
stop by just as I'm struggling with
another one of those salt-free, fat-free,
taste-free meals.

Is it my role (with a roll in my mouth, no less)
to amuse my mealtime visitor, God?
Must I cheerfully chew and try to answer
questions with a certain mumbling civility?

Some say a hospital experience can
demean one's dignity a bit, yet don't You think
I'm handling the mashed potatoes of my second
    childhood
much better than I handled the pureed carrots of my
    first?

Prayer for a Very Neat Visitor

She arranges my get well cards
in a precise row on the window sill,
then plucks the dead blossoms off my flowers;
she adjusts my blinds,
fluffs up my pillow,
straightens the sheets,
dusts off the TV,
hangs up my robe,
and places my slippers under the bed.
I pray, dear God, that You who have
enlightened this lovable child,
may continue to shower Your grace upon her
so that her new-found appreciation for tidiness
extends to her own room at home.

Prayer for a Surrogate Visitor

She's here to visit not me, but the patient in the
  next bed,
yet every time she comes in and sees me without a
  visitor
she'll pull up a chair
and spend five minutes or so
chatting with me, too.
So far I've learned that two of her children are
  married,
one of whom is six months pregnant,
her husband is four years from retirement,
and "doesn't life eventually turn out right?"
Does it, God?
For all of us?
Or for a few lucky ones who . . .
. . . who . . .
who make their own luck?
Is that it, God?
Has she made her own good fortune?
If so, why can't we all?
Why can't I, too?
Maybe what it takes
is going through life
pulling up a chair
and spending time
with people.

Prayer When Visiting Hours Are Over

What a difference a day makes.
(No, I'm not about to break into song)
I just want to point out to You—
and any saint who might care to eavesdrop—
the difference in my attitude
between yesterday and today.
Yesterday, when the announcement was made,
"Visiting hours are over,"
I still wanted company.
I was feeling sorry for myself—
and even sorrier to see my visitors shooed away.
Today, I was quite content to be left alone
with my thoughts. But I wasn't;
all day a steady stream of get well wishers
had come by—and rather than finding
the chatty recuperator of yesterday,
they found an aloof supine lump.

Do You suppose, God, as I continue
slogging my way toward perfection,
You could suggest a way for me
to cut down on these up-one-day,
down-the-next, mood swings?
Mind You, I don't want to be considered
a person who's "always predictable,"
but I sure wouldn't mind being thought of
as a person who's "always pleasant."

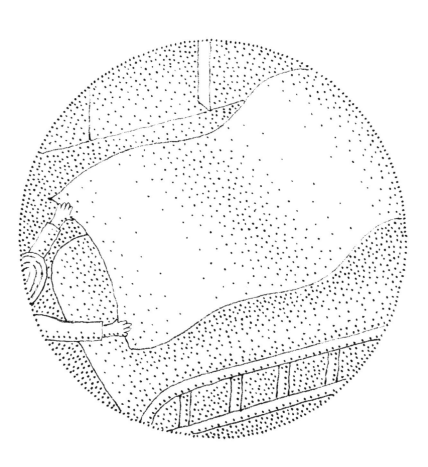

The Staff and the Stuff with which they work will doubtlessly have more impact on the patient than just about anyone or anything else that the hospital experience may present. After all, the medical personnel, these professionals and their procedures, are the reason we are in the hospital in the first place. We have come here so that these corporal caretakers may use their skills and techniques to bring us back, as nearly as possible, to the original us.

Now, since the original you is *an* original you, as you might have mentioned to God in the ID Band Prayer, how the staff and their stuff affects both your body and your spirit is critical. Sufficiently critical, I might add, that to keep our thoughts about staff to ourselves may not be the best thing to do. That might take us back, all the way back, to brooding—which, as we've said, is something we must try to avoid. And avoid it we certainly can. Especially since we have at our disposal a splendid sounding board on both day and night duty. God created the eternally engaging you. Now, engage God in conversation whenever a hospital staff member provokes either a question or a perception on your part. The question need not be a medical one. And your perception may not be about that person. It can be about yourself. And a reflection, a meditation, a prayer inspired by a doctor, nurse, X-ray technician need not be directly related to your hospital stay. This place, this time, is so right, so conducive to a heart-to-heart with Your Creator. And members of the hospital staff provide a splendid stimulus. They are a sure and serviceable conduit for a quick or a leisurely chat with God. So why not use them?

Prayer During the Taking of Blood

He stretches the skin on the inside of my arm,
taps a vein with his finger and
apologizes for any pain he may cause.
He needn't apologize, but I'm glad he has;
the fact is, it doesn't hurt at all.
Is this tall blond vampire incredibly proficient,
or am I just not as sensitive as I ought to be?
Which brings me to this thought, God:
> what if I could become sensitive enough
> to apologize beforehand for any pain
> I might cause someone?
> What if I were more aware of
> the consequences something I say or do
> might have, and so I'd begin by saying,
> "I don't want this to hurt, but . . ."?
> You know, God, I think I'll give it a try,
> yes, I'm going to give it a shot.
> Alerting someone to pain
> that might be unintentionally inflicted
> may actually prevent the unintentional pain—
> a lesson I have just learned from
> Your tall blond (compassionate) vampire.

Meditation While
a Doctor's Beeper Beeps

I've decided (BEEP) that I want to be important,
    too, God.
How do I go (BEEP) about it?
I want to be important (BEEP) enough
to be summoned
at the doggonedest times
and for any old (BEEP) reason at all.
Well, not quite any old reason, really.
I'd rather not (BEEP) be summoned
to eternity quite yet.
So what do You (BEEP) suggest, God?
What might make me as important
as my doctor (BEEP) seems to be?

Prayer for an Affectionate (?) Aide

Three days ago we had never met
and yet, in this blurry short period of time,
I have become her
  "hon,"
  "sweetie,"
  "dearie,"
  and "sugar."
And just now, God,
after she finished changing my sheets
she called me "precious";
she said, "now that should make you
feel cool and more comfortable, precious."
I can't remember ever being
called "precious" before;
not by spouse, nor by parent,
and although I'm sure You think it,
I can't say I've ever heard it from You, either.
So how have I endeared myself
in just 72 hours
to this expressive little woman?

Am I really "precious" to her?
If I am, please lavish
Your gratitude and mine upon her.
But if she's using the word
as one of those meaningless verbal hiccoughs,
surprise her by letting her know that
I am—
and she is—
and we are
indeed
really and truly precious . . .
just as she said.

Prayer for a Male Nurse

My nighttime Florence Nightingale has
a deep booming voice
and a mustache in need of a trim.
I've thought of asking him
how it feels to be a man in a job
that is considered stereotypically woman's,
but I sense it doesn't matter much to him,
for he dispenses TLC at these loneliest of hours
with as much grace and good humor
as the best of the other sex might.

Number me, God, among those myopic souls
who so often lapse into stereotyping people.
I suppose I have always thought
women had a chromosological lock on caring.
Abundantly bless my mustachioed nurse
for showing me that's just not so.

Meditation on a Redolent Nurse

She smells of smoke.
Should I tell her?
How could a caregiver—
and she seems to be an especially good one—
not care about herself?
She smells of smoke.
Should I tell her—
or will You?

 Which brings me, rather reluctantly,
 to this question: when do we impose
 ourselves on other people's lives?
 When do we express our feelings and
 opinions to people who haven't
 asked for them?
 When, if ever? Or never?
 You don't seem to shy away from
 letting us know how You feel.
 Should we, must we
 be more discreet than You?
She smells of smoke—
and I'm going to tell her.

Prayer for a Handholding Doctor

My roommate's doctor
holds my roommate's hand.
I can't recall *my* doctor
even shaking mine.
My roommate's doctor
strokes my roommate's hand.
Is that a sign my roommate's
illness is more severe
than I thought?
Or is it just that
I have always thought
doctors couldn't be all
that physically solicitous?
    Your touching people
    are special people—
    and I trust You touch them
    specially, too.

The Stat Prayer

If there's one bit of medical lingo
I've managed to pick up
both from listening to the staff
and being assailed by the paging system,
it's that "stat" means
   "right away,"
   "hurry up,"
   "on the double,"
which, in itself, translates to
   "a patient is in trouble."

Watch over, Eternal Guardian,
all those for whom
"stat" is broadcast.

I trust You will consider
this plea,
as You do all my prayers,
stat.

A Prayer for Charity and Trust

It's so easy for me—
and so awful of me—
to conclude that a doctor
not born under the Stars and Stripes
is of a different intellectual stripe,
not as knowledgeable,
not as well-educated
as American doctors.

I must, with Your help,
oh God, in *this* situation
I need all the help
You can give me,
squelch this feeling
that sometimes comes over me,
this distasteful unholy conclusion
that Dr. Kim and Dr. Panwabi
have come to this country
to learn and train on me.

I know, and truly believe,
that they are as *beloved* to You—
and therefore to me—
as every other one of Your creations.
It's trusting that they are
as *proficient* as other doctors
that I desperately need help with.
So *do* help, dear God,
I pray that You do.

Prayer for a Candystriper

Instead of leading cheers,
sharing a soda,
or breaking some boy's heart,
she's here warming mine,
reading me my favorite columns
from the local newspaper.

Would I have given up
any of my time at sixteen
to do this sort of volunteer work?
And they call this the Me Generation!
My Candystriper doesn't know that.
For her, it's the We Generation,
even though this particular We
are separated by more than forty years—
not to mention different values and lifestyles.

When I ask her why
she has volunteered
for this after-school activity,
she shrugs her pretty shoulders and says,
"I don't know . . . I suppose
it'll look good on my college application."

I pray, God, that this generous young lady
is looked upon kindly
not only by college admission officers,
but especially
by You.

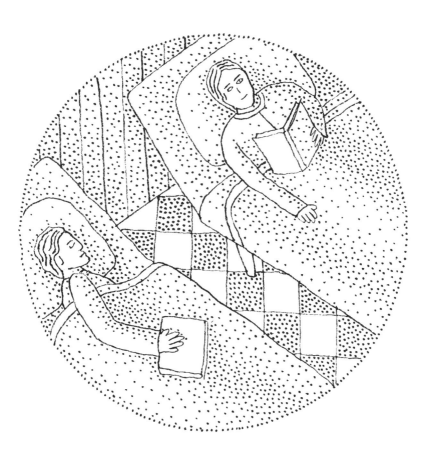

Our Mates on Nearby Mattresses may prove to be amusing or frightening, unforgettable or nondescript. Like it or not, like *them* or not, we do share a bond with our fellow patients that is deeper even than the mutual hospitalization we are undergoing. That bond is humanity . . . the inexplicably mysterious springing from the same unselfish source . . . the will of God.

The fact that there are uproariously different shapes under those johnnies, the fact that each bed is occupied by a person with his own distinct (sometimes outrageous) set of passions and priorities, the fact that some patients are more damaged of body and/or spirit than others, does not change the worth and the strength of the bond shared by us all.

Humanity's hold on us is inescapable.

And why, in God's name, should we *want* to escape it? After all, look how handy an access we have to appreciate the grandeur of God by seeing and sensing something wonderfully human about another human. And when that fellow human is only a few feet away, in a neighboring bed, that access to God couldn't be handier.

Meditation on a Momentary Friend

He came in late yesterday
and left before noon today,
hardly enough time to get his bed warm.
He was in "for tests," he said,
"more tests," he said, and in such
a strong and resolute baritone voice
that it suggested he had made peace
with himself,
with whatever his condition might be,
and with You.

Isn't that what we are all doing here, God,
not just here in the hospital,
but here on earth?
Aren't we here for, among other things,
"tests," "a few tests"?
Many of us who believe that to be the case
would like to be able to face those tests
with the strength and the resolve
that my momentary friend
appeared to have.
  I think I can come up with the strength;
  would You care to help me out with my resolve?

Prayer for Babblers

I've tried not to listen,
truly I've tried.
I've turned up Eyewitness News
and Jeopardy as loud as I could
yet I'm still drawn
to the babbler's babble,
the prolonged post-operative soliloquy
induced by one of those
state-of-the-art
anesthetic truth serums.
    I was about to ask You
    to watch over this babbler,
    but I realize You're doing just that,
    aren't You?
    So instead I'll ask You
    to watch over and guide
    all the rest of us babblers
    who, without the inducement
    of any drug whatsoever,
    go through life
    saying the silliest things,
    and believe them to be profound.

Prayer for the Person on the Phone . . . and Me

It's not the fact that
her phone keeps ringing
(rousing me out of my
umpteenth catnap of the day).

Nor is it the fact that
she keeps telling her callers
she hopes to be home by the weekend
(a hope I fervently share).

But it's that once
she's off the phone
(a rare moment indeed)
she proceeds to tell me
all sorts of negative things
about her many callers.

As I ask You, God, to point out
this shortcoming to her,
I also ask You to help me stop
pointing out other people's shortcomings
to You.

Prayer for a Professional Patient . . . and Me

I no sooner slip out of my slippers and slip
   under my sheet
than the man in the bed across from me asks me
   and tells me,
"Is this your first time here? It's my seventh."

I'll learn soon enough why
this is his seventh hospital stay
without asking—or even
appearing as though I am
interested knowing why.

Nonetheless, there's such a lilt,
such a bubbly cadence
in his voice that I find it
hard to believe this stay
or the prior six
have been justified.

Somewhere, God, between *his* boastfulness
   at being ill
and *my* chagrin and, yes, shame, at being here,
there must be an acceptance, a truthful
   acknowledgement
of one's illness—temporary or chronic.
No, not imagined.

May my roommate and I both find that measure
   of honesty
lest someday he feel compelled to ask me
   and tell me,
"Is this your second time here? It's my eighth."

Prayer for a Deep Sleeper

There are few acts more intimate,
I've come to conclude these days,
than watching someone sleep.

My roommate sits up for meals,
and an occasional visitor,
then quickly drops off into
a deep and seemingly painless slumber,
her chest heaving in rhythmic regularity.

There appear to be no dreams
disturbing her repose. Is that so?

Or is she having dreams,
but such pleasant dreams
that neither her mind
nor her body are disturbed?

I pray that the serenity
she seems to be enjoying
in sleep
can be maintained
when she awakes,
for I sense that it is
only in deep and constant sleep
that she finds
any peace at all.

Prayer for a Chocolate Lover

I know being a chocoholic
has a certain cachet these days,
but does she have to try
to lead everyone else
down the praline path?

Her visitors give her enough candy
to share with all the other patients,
all the staff, even other visitors.
And she *does* share,
telling us, as we grudgingly accept
yet another truffle,
of the wonders and powers chocolate enjoys.
And does *she* ever enjoy chocolate,
insisting all the while
that we enjoy it, too.

Oh yes, God, bless her generosity,
but let me say for what it's worth,
her continued generosity
will only add to my girth.

Meditation on an Old Lady's
Old Robe

One of Your more wonderful and overlooked
    gifts—
at least, overlooked by me,
is memory.
How many of the hours allotted me
have I spent in reverie,
harkening back to holiday tables,
and long-ago people
and indelible smells like damp musty wool?
Does a somewhat similar smell
of that tightly-cinched robe
stir *her* memory the same way, God,
bringing her back to a time of rich laughter
when she could open her gifts
with straight and supple fingers,
fingers which are straight and supple no more?
Who gave her the robe?
A husband? A grandchild?
Orange and brown aren't very feminine colors.
Could it conceivably be, God,
that the robe wasn't originally hers,
but his?
A husband's?
A son's?
Is she "wearing" a loved one
as she shuffles along the hospital corridors?
Is there any memory stronger
than the memory of love?

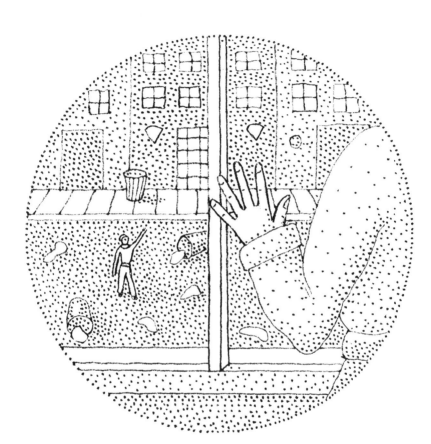

In Other Words in Other Wards (hospitals across the country have different expressions for their various divisions—wings and units and sections and annexes and wards) other bedridden folks are working to open up, or keep open, a channel of communication with God. For some people this may be an unusually taxing chore. Sedation, or an illness that impairs our thought processes, can make the simplest chat an enormous undertaking. True, God can make sense out of our garble. The fact remains a cogent conversation is often very difficult with a relative, let alone with our Creator, in some hospital quarters. We may find ourselves here for so many disparate reasons, some life-threatening, others life-giving, that the topics we talk to God about will vary widely, depending not merely on the state of our health, but on the location of our bed as well.

Prayer from an Intensive Care Unit

Every beat . . . every breath . . .
has a light . . . has a line . . . to
tell all those hovering
about me . . . how I am . . . *if*
I am.

And to think . . . that You . . .
loving You, hovering You, have
been monitoring every beat . . .
every breath long before
they attached . . . these
machines to me.

Can they read . . . not on those
screens . . . but in these eyes . . .
on this face . . . just how
at ease . . . just how at
peace . . . I am in Your care?

Prayer from a Geriatric Wing

He flaps his arms frantically
in giggly recognition.
A window and three floors separate us;
love and family unite us.
He's too young to visit,
but young enough to be able
to jump up and down
and wave to me unashamedly
from the messy sidewalk below.

Why messy, God?
Why does the world in which
he'll grow up have to be so messy,
with burger wrappers and soda cans
botching up the beauty You've ordained?

Yes, we, Your people
seem to be becoming
more and more beautiful in spirit,
caring for each other in very real,
not superficial, ways.
Grant, then, that we may extend
some of that caring
to the planet You've cared enough
to entrust to us.

Prayer from an Orthopedic Section

All those who say You don't answer prayers
need only look at me
and see that You *do*—
and *will* answer prayers
as passionate and pressing as mine.
I've asked You time and again
to keep me young—
and You have done just that . . .
to a degree.

Here I am, five decades along,
in my life's journey
and You have seen that
my mind is young enough
to play tennis and soccer
and baseball with the kids.

Just because my knees
aren't as young as my mind
shouldn't be seen
by some cynical so-and-so's
as a sign that
You *don't* answer prayers.

Prayer from a Maternity Ward

The squeals, the peeps, the wide-mouth howls
of these, Your latest spin-offs
are sweeter music to my ears
than any celestial choir
I could possibly imagine.

Don't get me wrong; I am most grateful
for his constant, reassuring, joyful noise,
but when one member of this impromptu chorus
fancies herself a 2 A.M. diva
(*every* 2 A.M.!)
in the crib alongside our bed,
give us the patience, God,
to appreciate the myriad sounds
You have chosen for Your creatures:
     the howls of nocturnal animals,
     the groans of suffering souls,
     the sighs of disappointed lovers,
     the hoots of preying birds,
     the coughs of nervous supplicants,
     and especially, most especially,
     the shrill soprano bawl
     of our hungry new-born daughter.

Prayer from an Emergency Room

It's taken me three hours
to get my badge of honor:
    six stitches
    for slicing
    my hand instead
    of my bagel.

These hours, these stitches
aren't apt to change my life
but a number of others,
broken and bloody,
who have been brought here
while I have been waiting
may, indeed, have their lives
dramatically altered.

Unplanned changes,
Painful veers off programmed courses.
Disruption.
Confusion.
Dear God, give those whose "emergencies"
will continue long after they have left this room
the will and capacity
to endure their prolonged trials.
And let us, who have shared,
in some measure, their
initial moments of anguish
always remember them in our prayers.

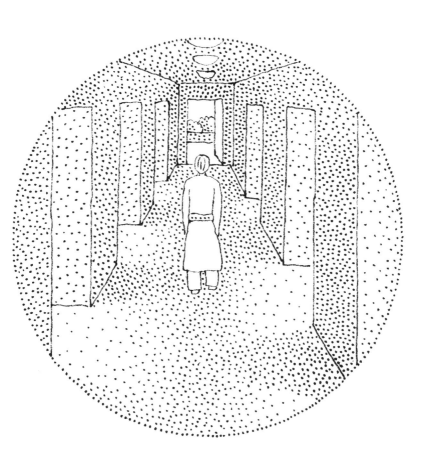

Up and About is a magnificent sensation, even when the reason we are finally up and about is to go off to yet another battery of tests. Just being able to leave our bed, our room at last and see some other green hospital walls can be a strangely uplifting experience. Occasionally, these new perspectives may offer us some new points of view as well. Points of view about what? About ourselves, perhaps. When and if we form some new thought, a fresh insight about ourselves—or about anything—in our new venue, it would be a shame to keep that thought to ourselves. Okay, the person in the elevator may not be keen on hearing it, but God surely is.

Solarium Meditation

Where is everybody?
I'd expect any of us capable
of getting here today
    (pushed,
    wheeled,
    or walked)
would like to spend time,
    sitting,
    lazing,
    warming our mending bodies
in this unusually-strong-for-this-time-of-year sun.
But take a roll call, God, and you'll hear
just a couple of "here's,"
mine, and ironically,
that of a man with burns on his face and shoulders.
Why aren't more of us here, lolling,
                basting,
                dozing,
                dreaming,
                growing.
That's it, good God, that's it!
In a solarium, smack dab in the sun,
plants and people grow.
Is that what we are avoiding?
Many of us, at this advanced stage of life,
don't want to believe that we can,
                we still,
                we must continue growing.

Meditation in the Hallway

For fifteen minutes a day,
so my doctor has decreed,
I can look at the world from a different vantage
    point,
from a chair in the hallway just outside my room.

And what does this new view offer me?
A parade of people needing help and receiving it:
patients, holding on to their nurses,
being helped along in their prescribed post-operative
    strolls;
a young man walking cautiously, supported,
in a couple of ways, by an IV unit on wheels;
one staff member helping another navigate
an occupied stretcher through the crowded corridor.

The lesson is obvious, even to me.
I, who have been a do-it-myselfer,
lo these many years,
even going so far as to decline help
when it has been offered,
might want to reconsider this attitude
in light of the
seemingly ordinary,
but probably extraordinary,
acts of help
that pass before me
fifteen minutes each day.

Prayer in an X-ray Room

Outside this room
only You can see through me
(at least I hope You're the only one).

Ah, but here, though not my innermost
thoughts and feelings (*Your* domain)
surely my innermost organs and their deficiencies
become strikingly apparent
to knowledgeable medical eyes.

Knowing the secrets of a person's body and/or soul
carries, I should think, an awesome responsibility.
Of course, *You* are up to that challenge.
I pray that the X-ray technician,
          my own doctor,
          and any other doctors
          with whom he consults
read me as accurately as You do.

Prayer from a Sitz Bath

All the spiritual things I have read
about water sanctifying and water purifying are fine,
but it's so good to find out again, God,
that water gets rid of one's external grunginess, too.
Here I sit for the first time in days
(or is it weeks?)
in a tub, pouring and dabbing water on myself
as giddily as a Sesame Street character.
And I'm not the least bit embarrassed
should a nurse pop in
and see me behaving like a naked ninny.
Certainly I appreciate water's purifying imagery,
but right now,
this minute,
I'm most grateful, God,
for the sheer fun
of the splashy stuff.

A Prayer for the Plaque People

Now that I can meander
through foyers and halls,
(nearly reached the lobby once
till I was told that's not allowed)
I see plaque after plaque
on wall after wall
giving heavily etched credit
to contributors to the hospital
and its many parts.

Some, I am sure, gave out of gratitude
or in memory of a loved one the hospital served
    well;
others, I suppose, gave as a tax deduction
or because they wanted to see their name up here in
    bronze.

Yet it really doesn't matter
what was their reason.
It really doesn't matter,
now does it God?
Motives are mortal,
and giving is just as divine
as *for*giving.
Whether You agree with this thought or not, dear
    God,
I hope You agree these Plaque People deserve Your
    blessing.

And One Final Prayer, as we plop ourselves into a wheelchair (in which we are, by hospital rule, obliged to sit until we are discharged at the front door—although some of us are totally capable of strolling, even strutting, out of here on our own). After our belongings have been gathered and placed on our lap, just before we tuck this book away we might want to take a moment to say:

> Yes, giving me this book
> was a lovely gesture
> but so many people
> have been so thoughtful
> during these days,
> during this adventure,
> why am I making
> special mention
> to You
> of this one gift?
>
> Perhaps, God, because
> it serves to remind me
> that one of the things
> we ought to be doing,
> whenever we get the chance,
> is reintroducing
> ourselves to You.